50 Cross Stitch Qu

Flowers and Fun

Bucilla/Plaid

Brighten your life with colorful blooms and carefree fun images with this big assortment of miniature cross stitch designs from Plaid's Bucilla Needlecrafts. With stitch counts of 35 by 35 or less, the designs are perfect for little gifts and accessories.

Garden Flowers

Stroll through this garden of blooms and pick your favorites for cross stitching a variety of projects. Finish them in tiny frames or attach them to clothing, linens, or other home accessories.

LEISURE ARTS, INC. • Maumelle, Arkansas

Orange Hibiscus

Stitch Count: 28w x 28h

Design Size: 2" x 2" on 14 count white Aida

Cross Stitch-2 strands

O	744	lt yellow
♥	743	yellow
⊠	742	dk yellow
2	740	orange
▨	947	dk orange
→	907	lt green
4	905	green
■	904	dk green

Backstitch-1 strand

╱	743	yellow
╱	838	brown

French Knot-2 strands

●	743	yellow

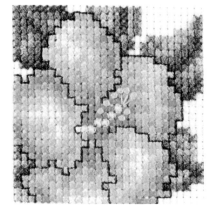

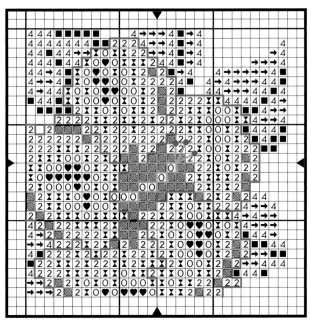

Pink Rose

Stitch Count: 35w x 35h

Design Size: 2½" x 2½" on 14 count white Aida

Cross Stitch-2 strands

O	963	lt pink
⊠	3716	pink
♥	962	dk pink
=	369	pale green
S	368	vy lt green
▽	320	lt green
⊓	367	green
♣	319	dk green
❘	890	vy dk green
·	blanc	white

Backstitch-1 strand

╱	309	vy dk pink
╱	890	vy dk green

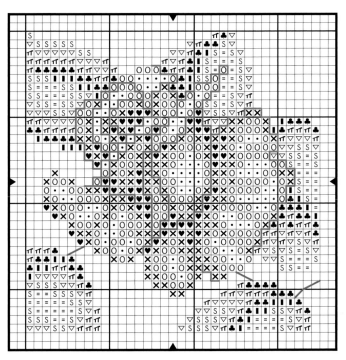

Hydrangea

Stitch Count: 35w x 35h

Design Size: 2½" x 2½" on 14 count white Aida

Cross Stitch-2 strands

◓	3822	lt gold
+	369	vy lt green
S	368	lt green
▽	320	green
¢	367	dk green
♣	319	vy dk green
=	747	sky blue
O	3811	vy lt teal
✕	598	lt teal
⊡	597	teal
▮	3810	dk teal

Backstitch-1 strand

╱	319	vy dk green
╱	3808	vy dk teal

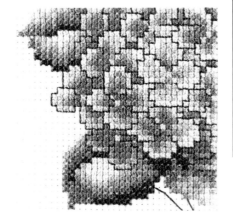

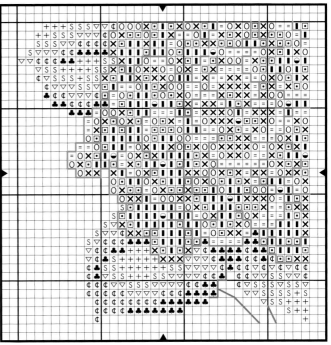

Camellia

Stitch Count: 35w x 35h

Design Size: 2½" x 2½" on 14 count white Aida

Cross Stitch-2 strands

=	3713	vy lt pink
O	761	lt pink
✕	760	pink
♥	3712	dk pink
¢	3078	yellow
◓	3822	gold
+	369	vy lt green
S	368	lt green
♣	320	green
⊡	367	dk green
▮	319	vy dk green

Backstitch-1 strand

╱	815	vy dk red
╱	319	vy dk green

3

Orchids

Stitch Count: 35w x 35h

Design Size: 2½" x 2½" on 14 count white Aida

Cross Stitch-2 strands

ᴗ	3609	vy lt fuchsia
₵	3608	lt fuchsia
ᴨ	3607	fuchsia
♥	718	dk fuchsia
O	3823	vy lt yellow
=	3078	lt yellow
✘	3822	lt gold
I	781	gold
+	772	vy lt green
▽	3348	lt green
♣	3347	green
·	blanc	white

Backstitch-1 strand

╱	718	dk fuchsia
╱	781	gold

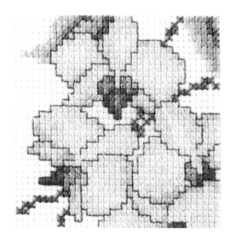

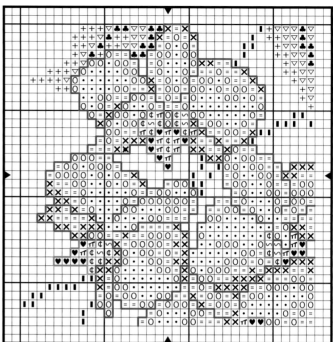

Daisy

Stitch Count: 35w x 35h

Design Size: 2½" x 2½" on 14 count white Aida

Cross Stitch-2 strands

▫	3078	vy lt yellow
✘	727	lt yellow
◖	726	yellow
ᴗ	369	vy lt green
▽	368	lt green
▣	320	green
♣	367	dk green
O	436	lt brown
I	801	brown

Backstitch-1 strand

╱	743	dk yellow
╱	369	vy lt green
╱	367	dk green

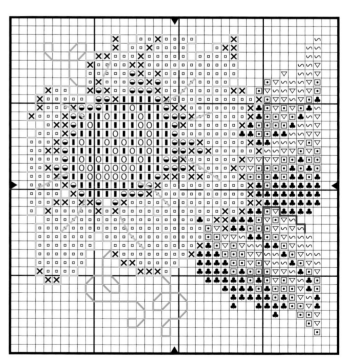

Daffodil

Stitch Count: 35w x 35h

Design Size: 2½" x 2½" on 14 count white Aida

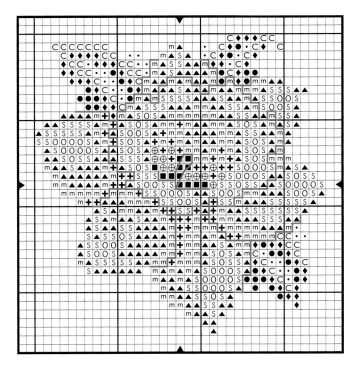

Cross Stitch-2 strands

S	3823	vy lt yellow
▲	3078	lt yellow
m	3822	vy lt gold
+	3821	lt gold
⊕	3820	gold
■	3852	dk gold
·	772	vy lt green
C	3348	lt green
◆	3347	green
●	3346	dk green
O	blanc	white

Backstitch-1 strand

/	801	dk brown

Heather

Stitch Count: 35w x 35h

Design Size: 2½" x 2½" on 14 count white Aida

Cross Stitch-2 strands

·	772	mint green
C	3348	lt green
♣	3347	green
◻	3346	dk green
≪	775	vy lt blue
☼	3325	lt blue
◑	334	blue
◪	322	dk blue

Backstitch-1 strand

/	895	vy dk green

Lavender

Stitch Count: 35w x 35h

Design Size: 2½" x 2½" on 14 count white Aida

Cross Stitch-2 strands

=	369	vy lt green
O	368	lt green
X	320	green
⊡	367	dk green
♣	319	vy dk green
·	3747	vy lt purple
+	340	lt purple
I	333	purple

Backstitch-1 strand

/	890	forest green
/	333	purple

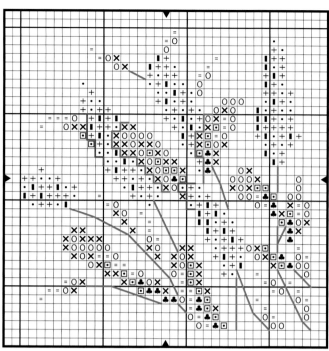

Hibiscus

Stitch Count: 35w x 35h

Design Size: 2½" x 2½" on 14 count white Aida

Cross Stitch-2 strands

=	963	vy lt pink
S	3708	vy lt melon
O	3706	lt melon
X	3705	melon
⊓	3801	dk melon
♥	666	red
I	321	dk red
▽	3348	lt green
♣	3347	green

Backstitch-1 strand

/	321	dk red

Backstitch-3 strands

/	741	orange

French Knot-3 strands

•	741	orange

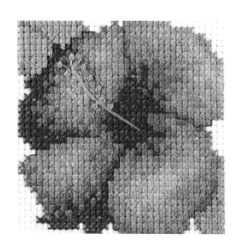

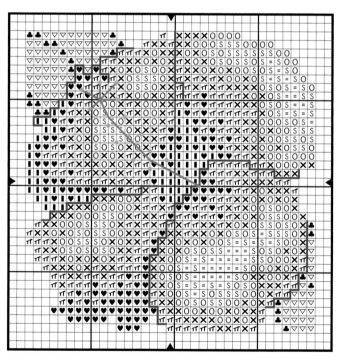

Kitschy Kitchen

Whether adorning dish towels and pot holders or framed for display on the wall or tabletop, these retro images will bring charm and humor to the heart of the home.

Time For Tea

Stitch Count: 35w x 34h

Design Size: 2½" x 2½" on 14 count white Aida

Cross Stitch-2 strands

☒	3846	turquoise
⊡	blanc	white

Backstitch-1 strand

╱	801	brown

French Knot-2 strands

●	801	brown

Lazy Daisy-2 strands

⬭	970	orange

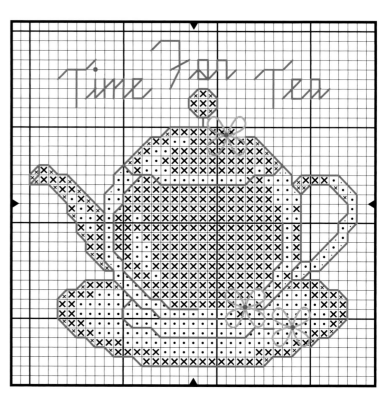

Strawberry Jam

Stitch Count: 35w x 34h

Design Size: 2½" x 2½" on 14 count white Aida

Cross Stitch-2 strands

⊙	3706	pink
■	666	red
⊟	955	vy lt green
m	954	lt green
♡	913	green
✚	912	dk green
◆	310	black
⊟	blanc	white

Backstitch-1 strand

╱	912	dk green
╱	310	black

French Knot-2 strands

●	666	red

Lazy Daisy-2 strands

⬭	743	yellow

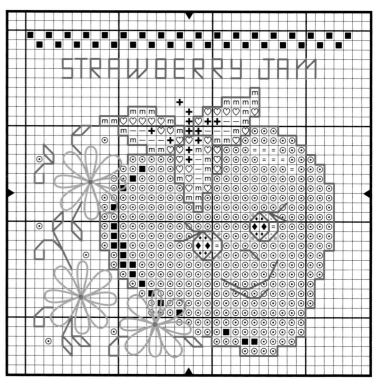

Hot Pots

Stitch Count: 35w x 34h

Design Size: 2½" x 2½" on 14 count white Aida

Cross Stitch-2 strands

★	743	yellow
♥	3801	lt red
2	666	red
♦	321	dk red
■	310	black
0	blanc	white

Backstitch-1 strand

/	912	green
/	310	black

French Knot-2 strands

•	743	yellow

Lazy Daisy-2 strands

◠	3801	lt red
◠	912	green

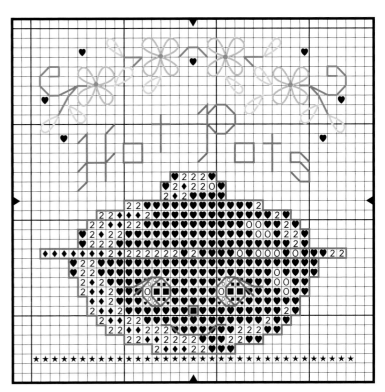

Red Rooster

Stitch Count: 33w x 35h

Design Size: 2⅜" x 2½" on 14 count white Aida

Cross Stitch-2 strands

●	321	red

Backstitch-1 strand

/	321	red

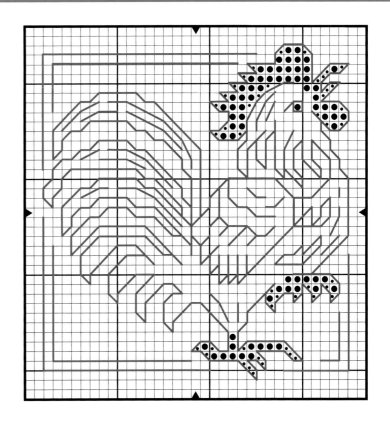

Mom's Kitchen

Stitch Count: 35w x 35h

Design Size: 2½" x 2½" on 14 count white Aida

Cross Stitch-2 strands

♥	743	yellow
O	955	vy lt green
⚡	954	lt green
▨	3839	blue

Backstitch-1 strand

/	911	green
/	3839	blue

French Knot-2 strands

•	743	yellow
•	3839	blue

Lazy Daisy-2 strands

⬭	3708	pink

Pear

Stitch Count: 33w x 35h

Design Size: 2⅜" x 2½" on 14 count white Aida

Cross Stitch-2 strands

♡	3078	vy lt yellow
=	727	lt yellow
◇	726	yellow
✕	725	dk yellow
⊘	369	lt green
☆	368	green
✦	320	dk green
#	434	brown
▫	blanc	white

Backstitch-1 strand

/	319	vy dk green
/	434	brown

French Knot-2 strands

•	725	dk yellow

Lazy Daisy-2 strands

⬭	3708	pink

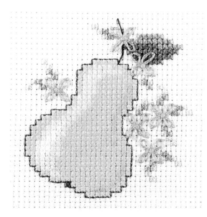

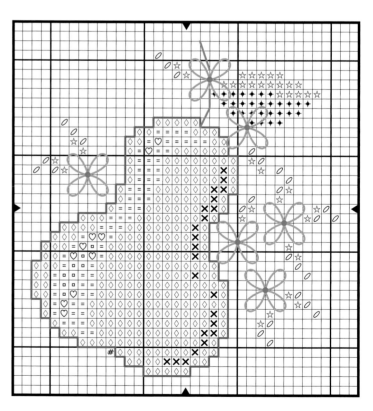

Vintage Silverware

Stitch Count: 33w x 33h

Design Size: 2⅜" x 2⅜" on 14 count white Aida

Backstitch-1 strand
/ 993   jade
/ 310   black

French Knot-2 strands
● 744   yellow
● 894   pink

Lazy Daisy-2 strands
⬭ 894   pink

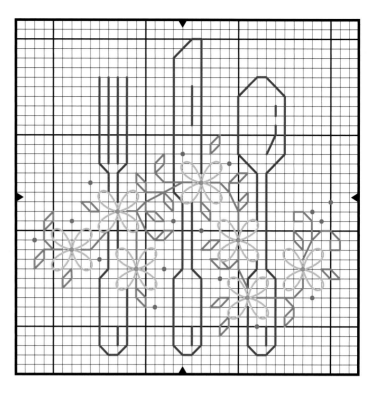

Wash the Dishes

Stitch Count: 35w x 34h

Design Size: 2½" x 2½" on 14 count white Aida

Cross Stitch-2 strands
♡ 3708   pink
✗ 310   black
▫ blanc   white

Backstitch-1 strand
/ 910   green
/ 310   black

French Knot-2 strands
● 740   orange

Lazy Daisy-2 strands
⬭ 742   yellow

Salt & Pepper

Stitch Count: 35w x 34h

Design Size: 2½" x 2½" on 14 count white Aida

Cross Stitch-2 strands

⊘	3840	lt blue
☒	3839	blue
◇	762	vy lt grey
#	415	lt grey
▫	blanc	white

Backstitch-1 strand

╱	912	green
╱	310	black

French Knot-2 strands

●	743	yellow
●	310	black

Lazy Daisy-2 strands

⬭	3801	lt red

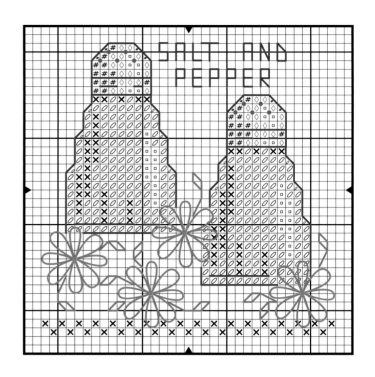

Cherries

Stitch Count: 35w x 35h

Design Size: 2½" x 2½" on 14 count white Aida

Cross Stitch-2 strands

⦀	3708	coral
⊠	3706	dk coral
2	3801	lt red
▨	666	red
♥	369	lt green
4	368	green
■	320	dk green
O	blanc	white

Backstitch-1 strand

╱	319	vy dk green
╱	666	red

French Knot-2 strands

●	725	yellow

Lazy Daisy-2 strands

⬭	3708	coral

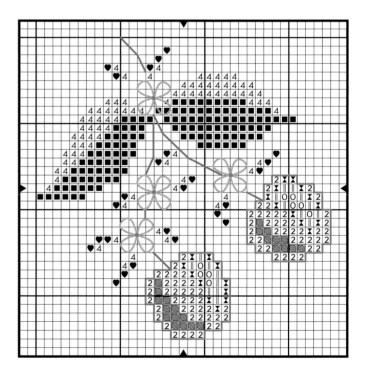

Floral Love

Beautiful flowers are the language of love! Whether representing romantic arrangements or whimsical gestures of joy, the bountiful blossoms in this collection are sure to please.

Whimsical Flower

Stitch Count: 34w x 35h

Design Size: 2½" x 2½" on 14 count white Aida

Cross Stitch-2 strands

⚊	742	dk yellow
➜	948	vy lt peach
2	3824	vy lt apricot
♥	3341	lt apricot
O	3340	apricot
▨	608	orange
◖	472	vy lt green
m	471	lt green
★	470	green
⠿	469	dk green
■	937	vy dk green

Backstitch-1 strand

╱	937	vy dk green
╱	898	brown

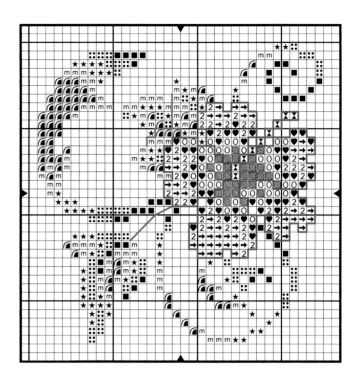

Daisy Heart

Stitch Count: 32w x 31h

Design Size: 2⅜" x 2¼" on 14 count white Aida

Backstitch-1 strand

╱	321	red

French Knot-2 strands

•	743	yellow

Lazy Daisy-2 strands

⬯	957	pink

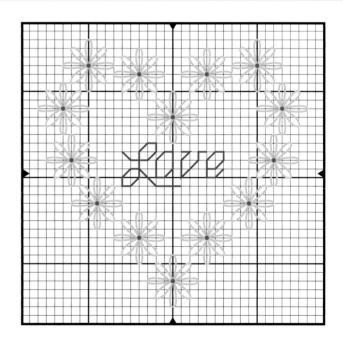

Flowers in Vase

Stitch Count: 33w x 34h

Design Size: 2⅜" x 2½" on 14 count white Aida

Cross Stitch-2 strands

·	3078	lt yellow
◇	726	yellow
✕	809	blue
★	321	red
∅	554	lt violet
C	553	violet
#	989	green
▲	987	dk green
●	310	black

Backstitch-1 strand

╱	987	dk green
╱	310	black

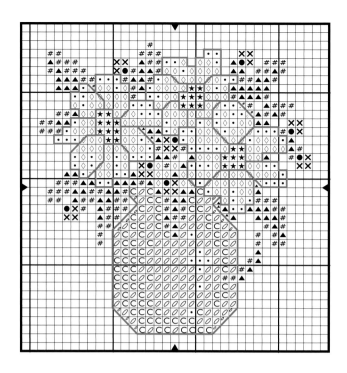

Stained Glass Floral

Stitch Count: 35w x 35h

Design Size: 2½" x 2½" on 14 count white Aida

Cross Stitch-2 strands

3	307	yellow
◆	972	vy dk yellow
0	350	coral
■	349	dk red
✳	553	purple

Backstitch-1 strand

╱	906	green

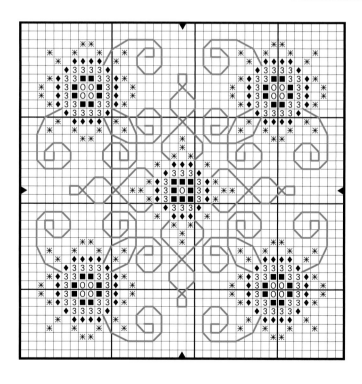

Red Floral

Stitch Count: 35w x 35h

Design Size: 2½" x 2½" on 14 count white Aida

Cross Stitch-2 strands

m	742	dk yellow
⁄	3708	lt melon
⚹	3706	melon
4	3801	dk melon
▨	666	red
O	907	lt yellow green
♥	906	yellow green
■	911	green
2	910	dk green
⊙	blanc	white

Backstitch-1 strand

⁄	898	dk brown

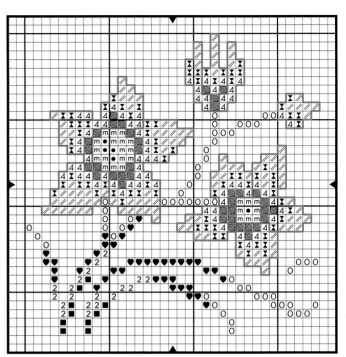

Blue & Orange Floral

Stitch Count: 35w x 35h

Design Size: 2½" x 2½" on 14 count white Aida

Cross Stitch-2 strands

▨	725	yellow
■	970	orange
O	907	lt green
♥	906	green

Backstitch-1 strand

⁄	906	green

Straight Stitch-2strands

⁄	970	orange
⁄	3845	turquoise

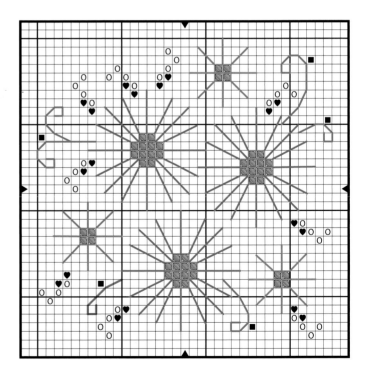

Tulip

Stitch Count: 30w x 35h

Design Size: 2¼" x 2½" on 14 count white Aida

Cross Stitch-2 strands

O	743	yellow
→	963	vy lt pink
4	957	lt pink
♥	956	pink
✕	907	lt green
2	906	green
■	905	dk green
▧	208	purple

Backstitch-1 strand

/	310	black

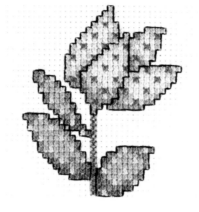

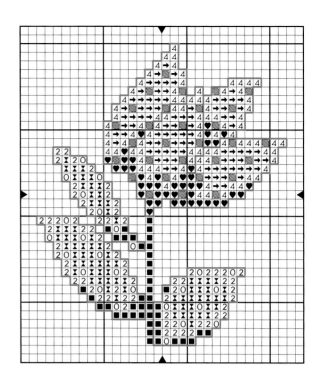

Striped Daisy

Stitch Count: 33w x 35h

Design Size: 2⅜" x 2½" on 14 count white Aida

Cross Stitch-2 strands

⌀	605	pink
✕	602	dk pink
▲	704	green
◇	727	yellow
●	972	dk yellow

Backstitch-1 strand

/	972	dk yellow
/	699	dk green
/	310	black

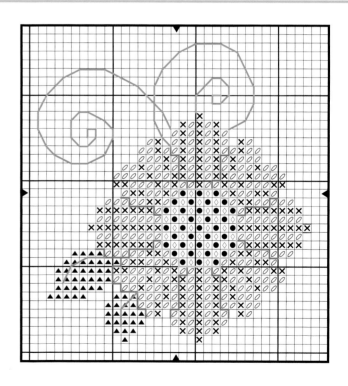

Fun Flower

Stitch Count: 35w x 35h

Design Size: 2½" x 2½" on 14 count white Aida

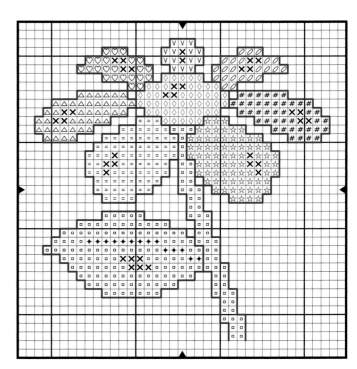

Cross Stitch-2 strands

◇	744	lt yellow
☆	742	yellow
⊘	957	lt pink
♡	956	pink
▫	907	green
◆	904	dk green
△	964	aqua
V	794	blue
#	3746	blue-violet
=	209	lavender
✕	blanc	white

Backstitch-1 strand

╱	310	black

Love

Stitch Count: 35w x 33h

Design Size: 2½" x 2⅜" on 14 count white Aida

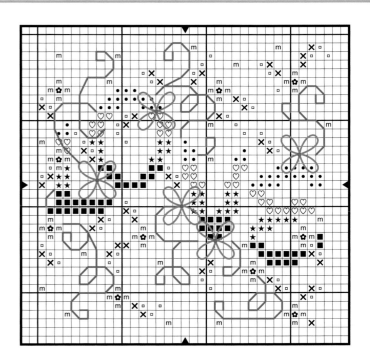

Cross Stitch-2 strands

●	899	lt pink
♡	335	pink
★	309	dk pink
■	326	vy dk pink
✿	743	yellow
▫	772	vy lt green
✕	3348	lt green
m	3840	blue

Backstitch-1 strand

╱	3347	green

French Knot-2 strands

●	743	yellow

Lazy Daisy-2 strands

⟠	3840	blue

Eat, Drink, Play!

This collection of easy-to-stitch summertime designs are bright and colorful. Enjoy stitching all designs from country birdhouses to your favorite fun-in-the-sun treats!

Birdhouse

Stitch Count: 35w x 35h

Design Size: 2½" x 2½" on 14 count white Aida

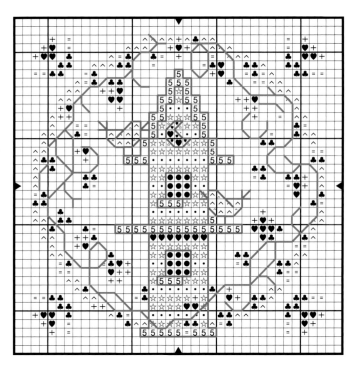

Cross Stitch-2 strands

⊡	3822	lt gold
☆	3820	gold
⊞	3716	pink
♥	321	red
⊟	989	lt green
♣	987	green
^	794	blue
5	3826	golden brown
●	310	black

Backstitch-1 strand

╱	987	green
╱	310	black

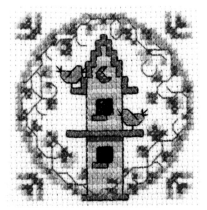

Birdhouse Row

Stitch Count: 36w x 37h

Design Size: 2⅝" x 2¾" on 14 count white Aida

Cross Stitch-2 strands

☆	726	yellow
4	894	lt pink
⊠	893	pink
✖	321	red
✳	989	green
●	987	dk green
♣	322	blue
⊙	208	purple
■	844	dk grey

Half Cross Stitch-1 strand

2	322	blue

Backstitch-1 strand

╱	844	dk grey

French Knot-2 strands

•	726	yellow
•	844	dk grey

Café

Stitch Count: 32w x 33h

Design Size: 2⅜" x 2⅜" on 14 count white Aida

Cross Stitch-2 strands

=	726	yellow
♡	304	red
⊘	907	lt green
✦	987	green
△	157	blue
V	738	tan
#	435	lt brown
◆	310	black
▫	blanc	white

Backstitch-1 strand

/	304	red
/	987	green
/	310	black

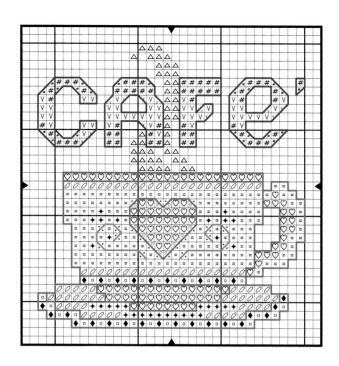

Roasting Marshmallows

Stitch Count: 35w x 35h

Design Size: 2½" x 2½" on 14 count white Aida

Cross Stitch-2 strands

=	745	lt yellow
♡	743	yellow
A	741	orange
✕	3801	dk melon
V	712	cream
✦	739	lt tan
⊘	436	vy lt brown
☆	435	lt brown
✶	434	brown
▫	blanc	white

Backstitch-1 strand

/	310	black

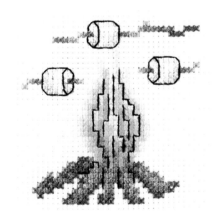

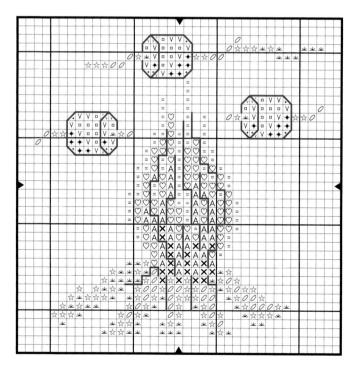

Teapot

Stitch Count: 34w x 30h

Design Size: 2½" x 2¼" on 14 count white Aida

Cross Stitch-2 strands

⊘	726	yellow
♡	304	red
V	907	lt green
♣	987	green
◇	809	lt blue
◆	798	blue
◻	blanc	white

Backstitch-1 strand

╱	798	blue
╱	310	black

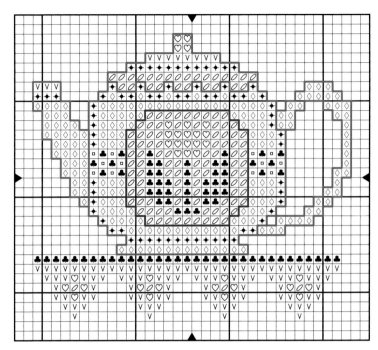

Teacup

Stitch Count: 25w x 25h

Design Size: 1⅞" x 1⅞" on 14 count white Aida

Cross Stitch-2 strands

▲	350	melon
·	3854	lt orange
O	912	green
✕	3766	turquoise

Backstitch-1 strand

╱	938	dk brown

Straight Stitch-1 strand

╱	3854	lt orange

Straight Stitch-2 strands

╱	938	dk brown

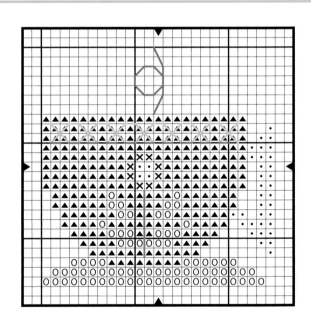

Popsicles

Stitch Count: 24w x 26h

Design Size: 1¾" x 1⅞" on 14 count white Aida

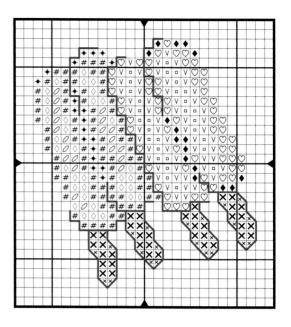

Cross Stitch-2 strands

⊘	963	vy lt pink
◇	3716	lt pink
#	962	pink
◆	961	dk pink
▫	754	peach
V	353	lt coral
♡	352	coral
◆	351	dk coral
✕	738	tan

Backstitch-1 strand

╱	801	brown

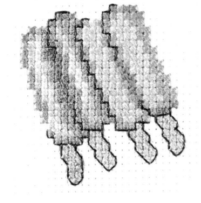

Sundae

Stitch Count: 28w x 27h

Design Size: 2" x 2" on 14 count white Aida

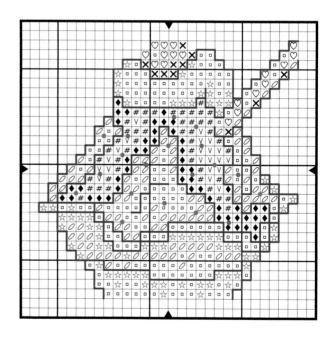

Cross Stitch-2 strands

♡	3733	pink
✕	3350	dk pink
⊘	712	cream
V	840	lt brown
#	839	brown
◆	838	dk brown
☆	762	lt grey
▫	blanc	white

Backstitch-1 strand

╱	838	dk brown

French Knot-2 strands

●	3733	pink
●	827	lt blue

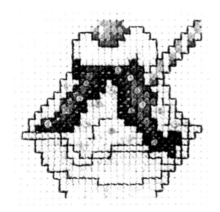

Banana Split

Stitch Count: 28w x 26h

Design Size: 2" x 1⅞" on 14 count white Aida

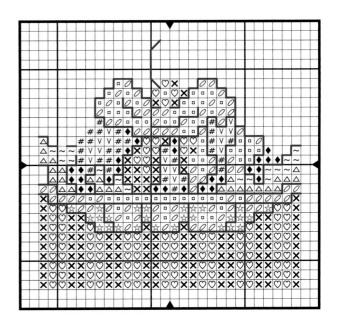

Cross Stitch-2 strands

~	3823	vy lt yellow
△	745	lt yellow
♡	3733	pink
✗	3350	dk pink
⊘	712	cream
V	842	lt brown
#	839	brown
◆	838	dk brown
☆	762	lt grey
▫	blanc	white

Backstitch-1 strand

╱	838	dk brown

Flip Flops

Stitch Count: 26w x 27h

Design Size: 1⅞" x 2" on 14 count white Aida

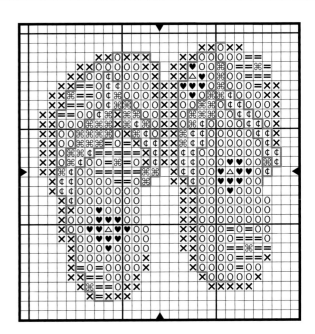

Cross Stitch-2 strands

♥	666	red
═	3820	gold
△	3348	green
O	209	lt purple
✗	208	purple
¢	3607	fuchsia
⌘	718	dk fuchsia

Backstitch-1 strand

╱	310	black

Frivolous & Fun

You'll find lots of reasons to smile with the fun images and kind sentiments expressed in this collection of mini designs.

I Love You

Stitch Count: 38w x 38h

Design Size: 2¾" x 2¾" on 14 count white Aida

Cross Stitch-2 strands

▪	957	lt pink
♡	956	pink

Backstitch-2 strands

╱	321	red

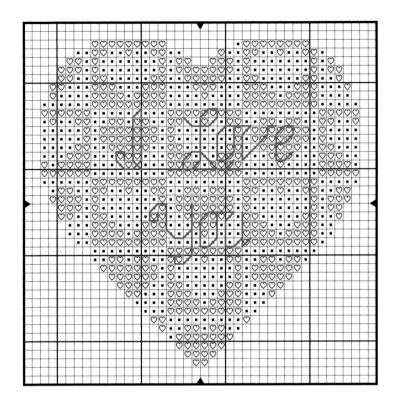

Sand Castle

Stitch Count: 28w x 28h

Design Size: 2" x 2" on 14 count white Aida

Cross Stitch-2 strands

♡	604	pink
✦	912	green
⊘	800	vy lt blue
Y	794	lt blue
A	3839	blue
◇	340	periwinkle
▫	677	vy lt gold
=	738	tan
✕	436	lt brown

Backstitch-1 strand

╱	3839	blue
╱	433	brown

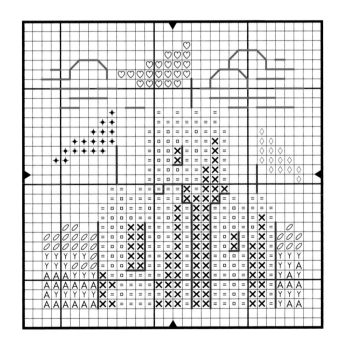

Thank You

Stitch Count: 34w x 35h

Design Size: 2½" x 2½" on 14 count white Aida

Cross Stitch-2 strands

+	3708	lt melon
⋈	3706	melon
✿	3801	dk melon
✳	743	yellow
⊡	742	dk yellow
⊛	704	green

Backstitch-1 strand

╱	3848	teal

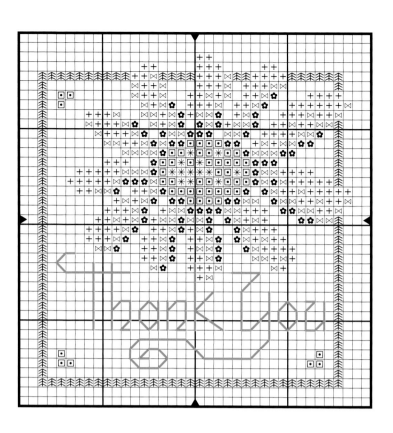

Babushka Doll

Stitch Count: 25w x 25h

Design Size: 1⅞" x 1⅞" on 14 count white Aida

Cross Stitch-2 strands

⊟	605	pink
6	3805	dk pink
0	772	lt green
✕	3766	turquoise
●	938	dk brown

Backstitch-1 strand

╱	912	green
╱	434	brown
╱	938	dk brown

French Knot-2 strands

●	912	green
●	938	dk brown

Lazy Daisy-1 strand

⬭	3805	dk pink
⬭	3854	lt orange
⬭	350	coral

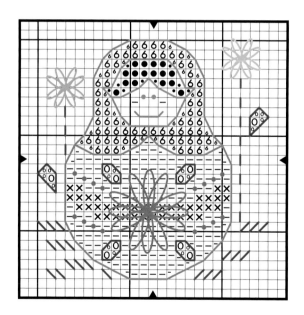

Mushroom

Stitch Count: 23w x 22h

Design Size: 1¾" x 1⅝" on 14 count white Aida

Cross Stitch-2 strands

▲	350	melon
⊡	772	lt green
■	912	green

Backstitch-1 strand

╱	350	melon
╱	912	green
╱	434	brown

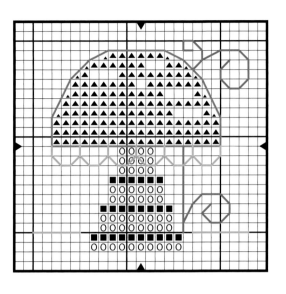

You Are My Sunshine

Stitch Count: 25w x 23h

Design Size: 1⅞" x 1¾" on 14 count white Aida

Cross Stitch-2 strands

⊟	605	pink
▲	350	coral
⊡	3854	lt orange

Backstitch-1 strand

╱	605	pink
╱	350	coral
╱	3854	lt orange

Backstitch-2 strands

╱	350	coral
╱	3854	lt orange

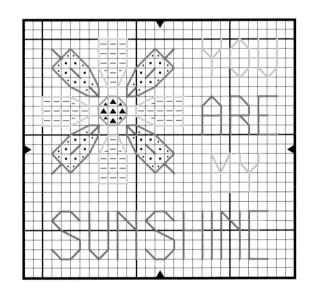

Bee Happy

Stitch Count: 25w x 25h

Design Size: 1⅞" x 1⅞" on 14 count white Aida

Cross Stitch-2 strands

⊡	3854	lt orange
▲	350	melon
☒	3766	turquoise

Backstitch-1 strand

╱	350	melon
╱	434	lt brown
╱	938	dk brown

French Knot-2 strands

●	938	dk brown

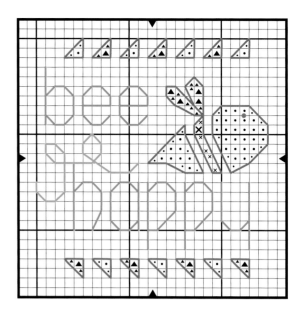

Be Brave

Stitch Count: 25w x 26h

Design Size: 1⅞" x 1⅞" on 14 count white Aida

Cross Stitch-2 strands

⊡	772	lt green
☒	3766	turquoise

Backstitch-1 strand

╱	938	dk brown

Backstitch-2 strands

╱	938	dk brown

Lazy Daisy-2 strands

⬭	605	pink
⬭	772	lt green
⬭	3766	turquoise

Be Free

Stitch Count: 25w x 25h

Design Size: 1⅞" x 1⅞" on 14 count white Aida

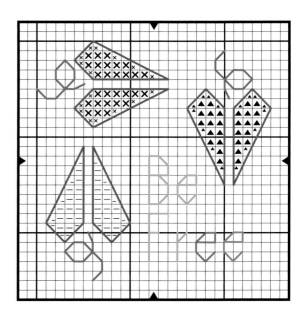

Cross Stitch-2 strands

⊟	605	pink
▲	350	melon
☒	3766	turquoise

Backstitch-1 strand

╱	912	green
╱	434	brown

Backstitch-2 strands

╱	3805	dk pink
╱	350	melon
╱	912	green
╱	3766	turquoise

Unicorn Dreams

Stitch Count: 29w x 35h

Design Size: 2⅛" x 2½" on 14 count white Aida

Cross Stitch-2 strands

⊡	819	lt pink
⊠	3326	pink
◇	3805	dk pink
••	718	fuchsia
△	3846	turquoise
■	310	black

Cross Stitch-1 strand

☆	743	yellow

Backstitch-1 strand

╱	3326	pink
╱	3804	vy dk pink
╱	915	dk fuchsia
╱	310	black

General Instructions

HOW TO READ CHARTS

Each chart is made up of a key and a charted design on which each square represents a stitch. The symbols in the key tell which floss color to use for each stitch on the chart. The key will indicate the stitch and how many strands to use.

 A square filled with a full-size symbol should be stitched as a **Cross Stitch**.

 A reduced symbol in a corner of the square is usually stitched as a **One-Quarter Stitch**. A reduced symbol in a corner of the square should be stitched as a **Three-Quarter Stitch** when a Backstitch crosses two squares.

Three-Quarter Stitch

No Stitch

 A straight line should be stitched as a **Backstitch or Straight Stitch**. The color key will indicate which color to stitch.

 A large dot should be stitched as a **French Knot**.

 An oval should be stitched as a **Lazy Daisy Stitch**.

Sometimes the symbol for a Cross Stitch will be partially covered when a Backstitch, Straight Stitch, French Knot, or Lazy Daisy Stitch crosses that square.

GETTING STARTED

Preparing Fabric

Cut your fabric at least 3" larger on all sides and overcast the edges. It is better to waste a little fabric than to come up short after many hours of stitching.

Working with Floss

To ensure smoother stitches, separate strands; then, realign them before threading the needle. Keep stitching tension consistent. Begin and end floss by running under several stitches on the back; never tie knots.

Where to Start

The horizontal and vertical centers of each charted design are shown by arrows pointing to the center. You may start at any point on the charted design, however, it is best to center the design on the fabric. To locate the center, fold the fabric in half top to bottom and then again left to right.

On the charted design, count the number of squares (stitches) from the center of the chart to where you wish to start. Then, from the fabric's center, find your starting point by counting out the same number of fabric threads (stitches).

HOW TO STITCH

Always work Cross Stitches, One-Quarter Stitches, and Three-Quarter Stitches first; then add the Backstitch, French Knots, and Lazy Daisy Stitches. When stitching, bring the threaded needle up at 1 and all odd numbers and down at 2 and all even numbers.

Cross Stitch: For horizontal rows, work stitches in two journeys *(Fig. 1)*. For vertical rows, complete each stitch as shown *(Fig. 2)*.

Fig. 1

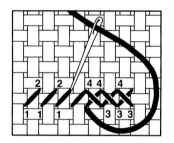

Fig. 2

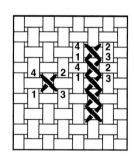

One-Quarter Stitch and **Three-Quarter Stitch:** Stitch 1-2 is the One-Quarter Stitch *(Fig. 3)*. When stitches 1-4 are worked in the same color, the resulting stitch is called a Three-Quarter Stitch.

Fig. 3

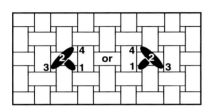

Backstitch: For outlines and details, Backstitch should be worked after the design has been completed *(Fig. 4)*.

Fig. 4

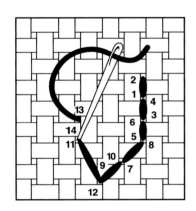

Straight Stitch: Bring the needle up at 1; go down at 2 *(Fig. 5)*.

Fig. 5

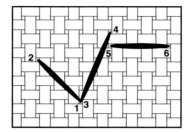

French Knot: Bring the needle up at 1. Wrap the floss twice around the needle. Insert the needle back in the same hole and tighten the knot. Then pull the needle through the fabric, holding the floss until it must be released *(Fig. 6)*.

Fig. 6

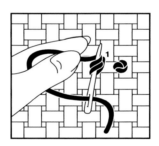

Lazy Daisy Stitch: Bring the needle up at 1 and make a loop. Go down at 1 and come up at 2, keeping the floss below the point of the needle *(Fig. 7)*. Pull the needle through and go down at 3 to anchor the loop, completing the stitch.

Fig. 7

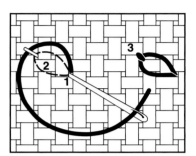